GLENN RILEY'S
Serious Shred

GET YOUR FINGERS TO PLAY
WHAT'S IN YOUR HEAD

Alfred Music Publishing Co., Inc.
P.O. Box 10003
Van Nuys, CA 91410-0003
alfred.com

ISBN-10: 0-7390-8609-X (Book & DVD)
ISBN-13: 978-0-7390-8609-4 (Book & DVD)

Cover guitar courtesy of Schecter Guitar Research
Author photo courtesy of Glenn Riley

 Alfred Cares. Contents printed on 100% recycled paper.

Contents

TUNE UP

In the DVD menu, select Tuning. It will take you to a page where you will hear an audio track that will play each string several times, starting with the 1st string, high E. Compare your strings to this audio track to get in tune with the DVD.

A NOTE ABOUT THE VIDEO

The DVD video corresponds to lessons in the book and the two are intended to be used together. Video lessons included on this DVD were filmed at various times over the period of a year; thus, you will note wardrobe and lighting changes from lesson to lesson.

Introduction

If you have been playing long enough to feel limited by what you know and what your fingers can do, the Serious Shred DVDs and books are for you. You have developed some lead guitar chops and know some scales and lots of chords, but would like to be able to play like the killer shredders you have heard. Each DVD/book combination in this series features a monster shredder guitarist teaching the left- and/or right-hand techniques and musical concepts you need to master to become the shredder you want to be. You'll be learning from the best, and will be inspired by the amazing demonstrations of licks and exercises in the video.

The optimum learning experience with the Serious Shred DVD/book series is to watch the video, guitar in hand ready to play, with the book open in front of you. Numbers will be displayed on your television or computer screen, directing you to licks and exercises in the book that include standard music notation, TAB, and chord or scale fretboard diagrams. Stop the video any time you need to practice an example. To ensure the effectiveness of the training offered here, master each lick or exercise before continuing on to the next lesson.

To make it easier for you to choose the appropriate Serious Shred DVD and book, they have been categorized into levels that are explained below.

ESSENTIAL

This level assumes you can read TAB and/or standard music notation, and know how to read chord and scale fretboard diagrams. You know all of the basic open-position chords and are ready for barres and other movable chords. You have some familiarity with the pentatonic scale, and are ready to learn a number of alternate positions in which it can be played. You're ready to master fundamental techniques like hammer-ons, pull-offs, alternate picking, and even some more specialized techniques, such as palm muting, bending, legato, vibrato, fingerstyle, tapping, and sweep picking. You also have the music theory background needed to begin learning the modes of the major scale and incorporate them into your soloing.

ADVANCED

To begin at this level, you should have all of the skills and knowledge developed at the ESSENTIAL level and are ready to explore more advanced techniques and concepts. You have the musical understanding needed to learn all the different types of 7th chords, plus extended and altered chords in a variety of voicings. You're ready for advanced applications of sweeping, tapping, harmonics, and whammy bar techniques. Your ready to explore topics such as phrasing, multi-finger tapping, Hendrix-style chord embellishments, and more.

ABOUT GLENN RILEY

G.I.T. graduate Glenn Riley started playing guitar at the age of 12. He resides in Baltimore, Maryland, where he has been teaching and performing since 1991. Glenn is the author of *Jam Guitar: Rock* (23230), *Progressive Rock Guitar* (#22547), *Rock Lead Guitar Solos* (#21959), and the co-author of *7-String Guitar Styles* (#21892), all published by the National Guitar Workshop/Alfred. Glenn is an instructor for the National Guitar Workshop and also Dayjams, the rock music day camp, for which he authored the bass guitar curriculum.

Bending

One of the most common techniques used in electric rock guitar soloing is a technique called *bending*. Bending adds expression to your playing and serves up some ear-grabbing emotion. I'm going to cover the basic concept and technique of bending the strings, including *unison bending*, *harmonic bends*, and *pre-bends*, as well as the *bend-and-release* technique.

The Whole-Step and Half-Step Bends

The idea here is to change a note so that it sounds a whole step, or two frets, higher. For example, play the G on the 8th fret of the 2nd string and then bend it up so it sounds like the A on the 10th fret. This is called a whole-step bend.

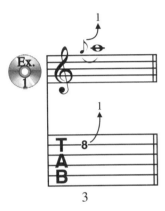

When executing this bend, use your 3rd finger to fret the note, and the 1st and 2nd fingers to help push. Also, your thumb can be wrapped over the top of the neck for some balance and reinforcement. It's important to make sure the bend doesn't fall short of the targeted pitch. Be sure not to bend too much, as that would also make things sound sour. It's a good idea to play the pitch you're targeting with your bend first, at its usual fret, then go back to the note you're bending, and bend up to it. For example, play the A on the 10th fret, then bend the G up to match the pitch you just played.

Let's try a half-step bend. We'll play the 7th fret, 3rd string with the 3rd finger and bend it up just a half step. The same principles as with the whole-step bend apply.

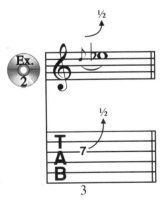

Unison Bends

In a unison bend, the goal is to have one note played normally (no bend), accompanied by a bend up to the same note on another string. The two strings are played simultaneously. Play an E note at the 5th fret, 2nd string, with your 1st finger, and a D note on the 7th fret, 3rd string, played with your 3rd finger. Strike both strings together and then bend the 3rd string D note up a whole step to E. The 2nd string is not being bent, but you're bending the 3rd string to sound like the 2nd string.

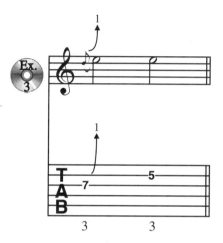

Here's a really cool lick using that technique.

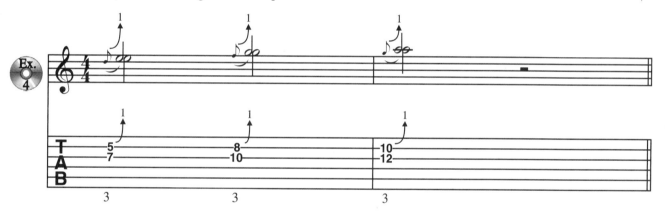

Pre-Bends

Pre-bending is bending the note before striking the string. Then, we strike the string and release the bend. Below is a whole-step pre-bend. Bend the D-note on the 7th fret of the 3rd string up a whole step so it will sound an E, then strike the string and release it back down to D. You can do the same thing with a half-step bend. Bend first, then play and release.

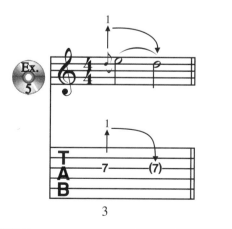

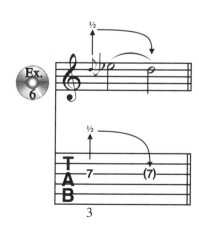

HARMONIC BENDING

This type of bending creates harmony and thick, full, big, fat sounds. We strike two strings and bend only one of them, and the two sounds are heard together. In the example to the right, the D note on the 7th fret, 3rd string is bent up to E with the 3rd finger, while the 4th finger holds the G-note on the 8th fret, 2nd string. Both strings are struck together at the same time, while only the 3rd string is bent.

You'll get a country effect if you bend the lower note more slowly, but for the rock sound just go right into the bend.

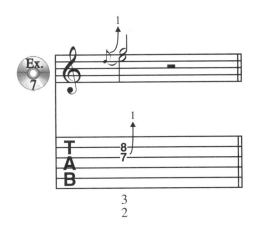

BEND-AND-RELEASE

This is a great melodic tool for your soloing. Try bending the 3rd-string D note up to the E note and without stopping the sound, release it back down to D.

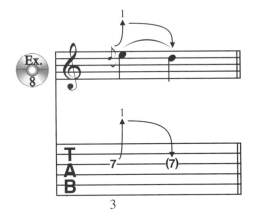

Now, try going back and forth. See how long you can make it last.

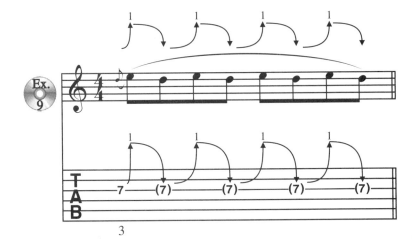

Do some bending and try improvising with it. That's the best thing to do; experiment and let it take you where it takes you.

Legato

Legato means to play smoothly, without a lot of separate attacks. One of the easiest ways to play this way on the guitar is to use lots of hammer-ons and pull-offs, where we pick one note and then play the next, or even the next few notes, with the left hand alone.

THREE-NOTE-PER-STRING G MAJOR SCALE

Below is a three-note-per-string G Major scale, starting at the 3rd fret of the 6th string. Ascend the scale using legato. Instead of picking each note, pick the first note and then hammer on the next two.

To descend, pick the first note and pull off to the next two. Make sure you don't lift your fingers straight up; get some friction between your fingertip and the string by pulling down a bit, too. Pick just the first note of each string.

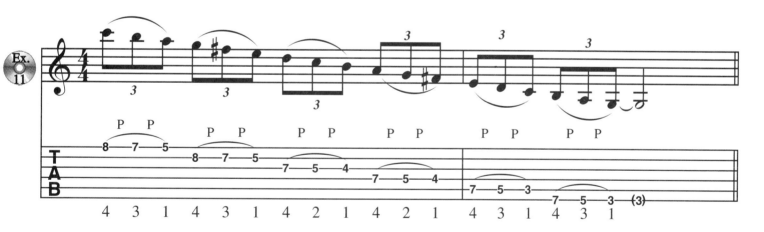

Legato Licks

This lick uses the notes of the E Natural Minor scale played entirely on the 4th string. There's a four-note pattern in which the 1st finger slides down to the last note, following the hammer-on and pull-off. Only the first note of each four-note group is picked.

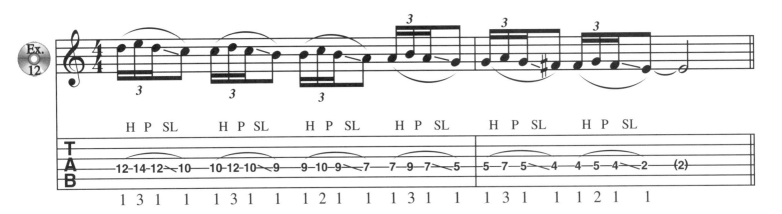

The hammer-on is emphasized in this next lick. It uses a cluster of six notes, which is phrased with a triplet feel. The next set of six starts with the last string played. This is a pattern-based lick.

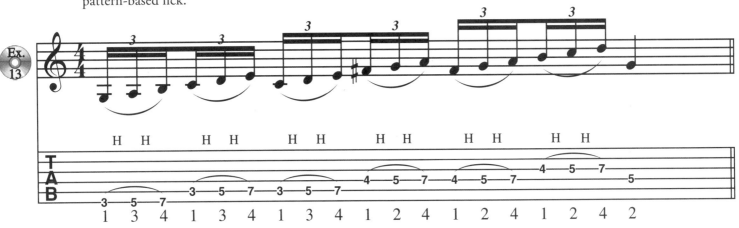

This lick is all about the pull-offs. There are descending three-note groups over three strings, ending on the D note. You can continue using this pattern until you arrive at the low G note on the 6th string.

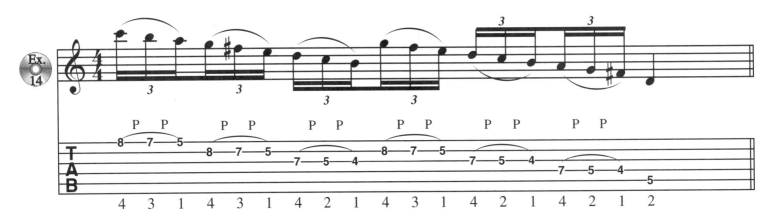

This crazy lick is a combination of hammer-ons, pull-offs, and slides. Notice that when changing to a new string, you'll be hammering-on to the first note; you don't want to interupt the legato flow of the lick by picking the string.

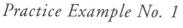

If you have trouble with this one, break it down into small snippets. Work on a small bit and add a few more notes at a time, until you have the entire lick memorized.

Legato is a great technique to mix into your soloing. Have fun!

EXTRA LEGATO PRACTICE

Practice Example No. 1

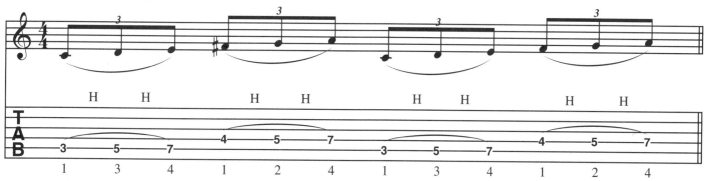

Practice Example No. 2

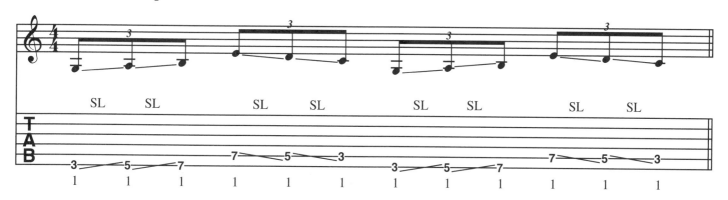

Vibrato

The vibrato technique is an awesome way to add a vocal-like dynamic to your soloing. It gets your guitar singing and crying. Basically, vibrato is playing a note and rocking it back and forth slightly, kind of like bending, but not perceptibly changing the pitch like you would in a bend. In this lesson, we'll check out how and when to use vibrato!

Applying Vibrato

Try playing a C-note at the 13th fret of the 2nd string using your 3rd finger. It will help to have your thumb wrapped over the top of the neck and your 1st and 2nd fingers balancing and supporting your 3rd finger on that same string.

Play the note and gently pull the string toward the floor with your fingers, and then let the string return by relaxing your hand. Now, push the string up just a little. Ultimately, you want to go back and forth.

Don't change the pitch very much; the idea is to create a wave-like effect and to increase sustain.

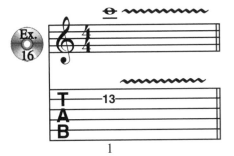

Licks with Vibrato

This lick starts and ends with vibrato applied to bent notes. Use your 3rd finger for both the bending and the vibrato.

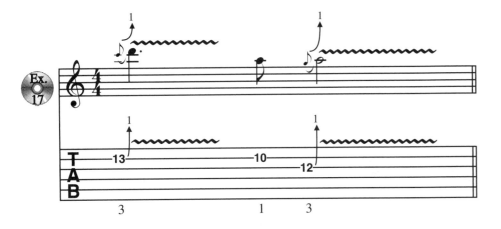

In this legato lick, you'll execute the vibrato with two different fingers. Use the 3rd finger to play vibrato on the bent note, and then after the hammer-ons and pull-offs, use your 1st finger to play vibrato on the last note.

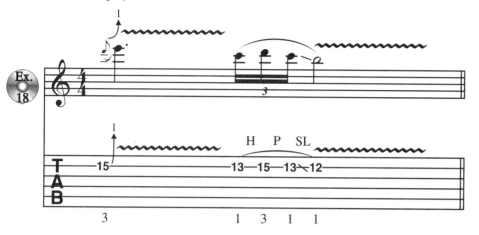

This lick provides an opportunity to try vibrato with different fingers. It's all on the 2nd string. Experiment by using your 1st, 2nd, 3rd, and even your 4th finger to see which you like best. Ultimately, you want to be comfortable executing vibrato with any finger.

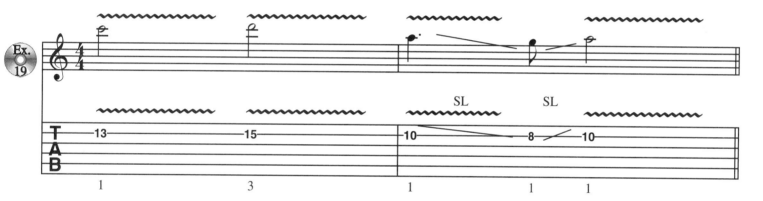

Vibrato is an awesome technique to have in your soloing toolbox. It will help you be a more expressive guitarist. Make sure you're always working on your vibrato, and have a great time.

Extra Practice with Vibrato

Example No. 1

Example No. 2

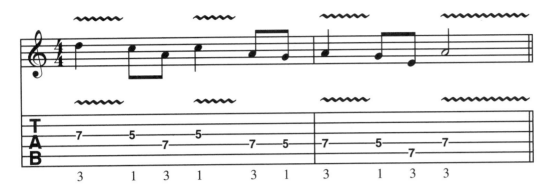

Example No. 3

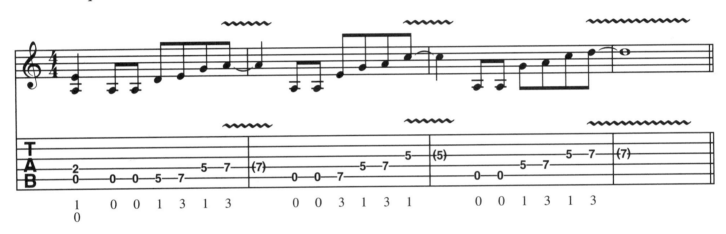

Strumming Logic

In this lesson, you'll learn how to strum with downstrokes and upstrokes. Most of the examples in this lesson use a technique called scratching, or chucking, and there's a strumming song for you to play in the last exercise. We'll start with quarter and eighth notes and work our way up to sixteenths. If you never knew how or which way to strum the strings, this lesson will really help you out.

DOWNSTROKES AND UPSTROKES ON MUTED STRINGS

Your fretboard hand should be touching the strings of the guitar lightly, so when you strum the strings, the sound is deadened.

When you listen to music and tap your foot, it goes down–up–down–up–down–up.

When your foot hits the floor, strike the strings with a downstroke, and then try an upstroke when your foot's coming up.

Practice Downstrokes and Upstrokes

This first exercise goes through a set of downstrokes, a set of upstrokes, and then alternates down–up–down–up, all on the beat.

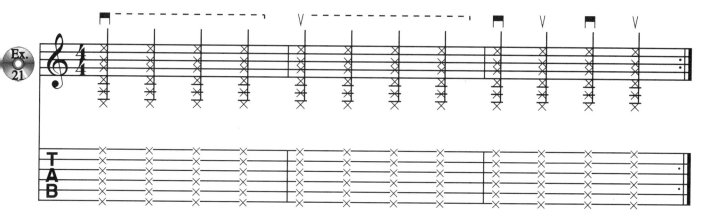

Isolating Upbeats and Upstrokes

This next example brings to mind funk or reggae, because it is all about the off-beat. The idea here is to strum the strings when your foot comes off the floor on the upbeat. Try strumming with an upstroke each time your foot comes off the floor.

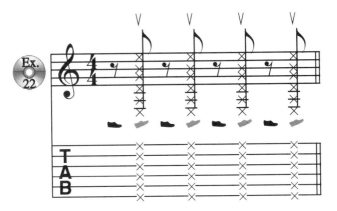

Now try doing both down and upstrokes with your pick. Remember, your pick should be synchronized with your foot.

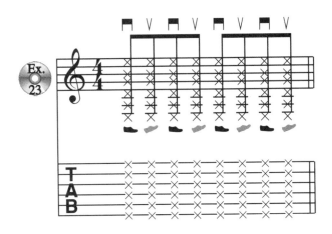

For some rock stuff, you want to play all downstrokes both on the down and the upbeats.

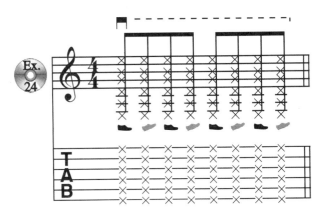

Now we'll combine all three ways of strumming. We'll mix downstrokes and upstrokes, and then we'll use downstrokes on both parts of each beat.

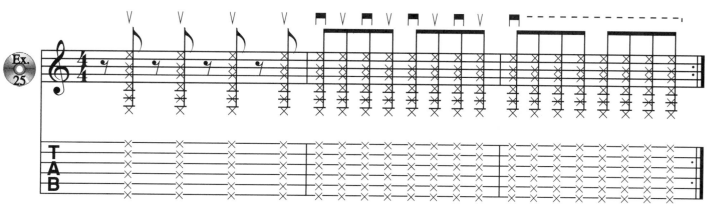

COMBINING QUARTER-NOTE AND EIGHTH-NOTE STRUMS

This next exercise combines quarter notes and eighth notes. Your pick should be perfectly synced with your foot for the example. Experiment with different combinations, or whatever feels natural to you.

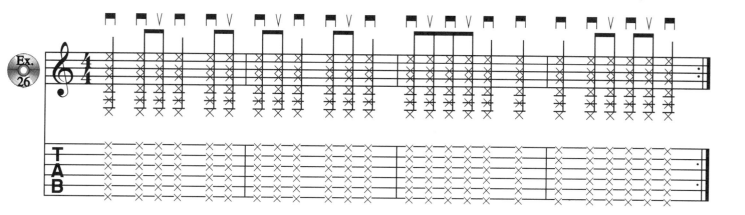

SIXTEENTH-NOTE STRUMMING

Sixteenth notes divide the beat into four equal parts. Tap your foot and strum an even four times for each beat.

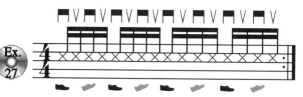

Four strums per beat

Notice the down–up–down–up strumming pattern.

The Gallop

What I think of as "the gallop" is a very common rock rhythm. Out of the four sixteenth-note attacks possible in each beat, remove the second to get the "gallop" rhythm. There are two different ways to strum this pattern, as shown below.

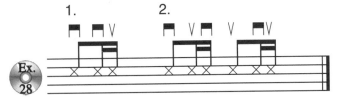

Play the exercise.

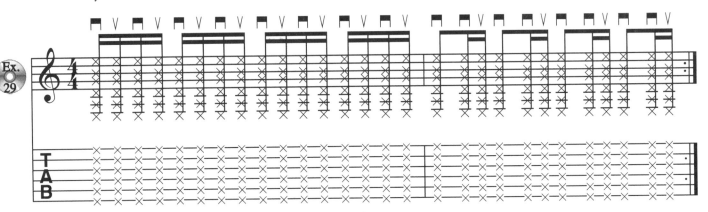

COMBINING ALL OF THE STRUMMING PATTERNS

This example using root-6 power chords A, G, F, and E will help you practice strumming the rhythms discussed in this lesson. This starts pretty easy, but gets more difficult toward the end.

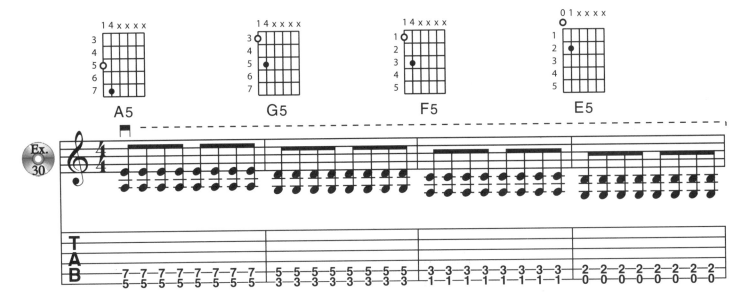

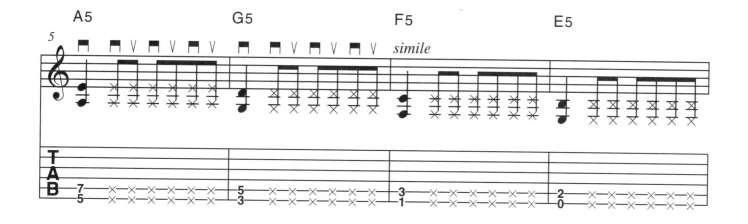

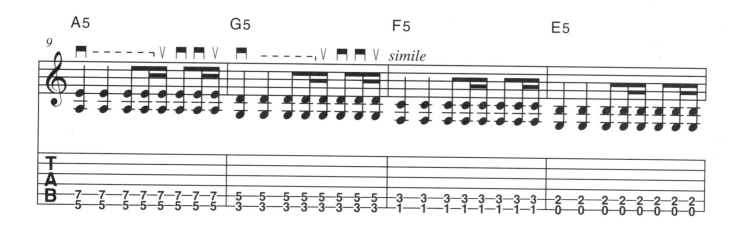

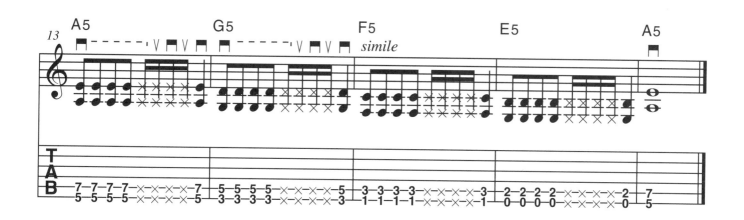

Extra Strumming Practice

Example No. 1

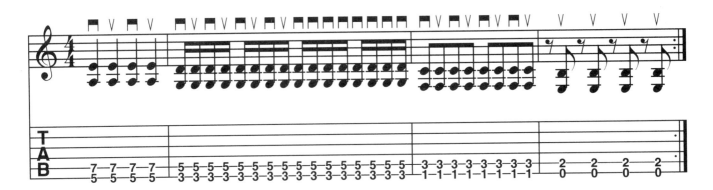

Example No. 2

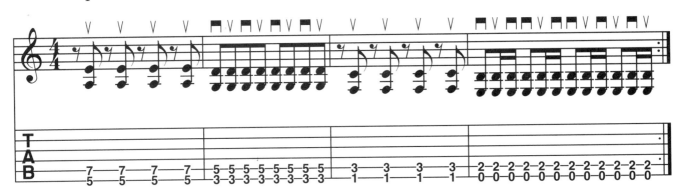

Triplets

If you're into bluesy classic rock, this lesson will be right up your alley. We'll cover the triplet rhythm using some easy single-note scale examples, some power chords, and some licks that you can use to solo or improvise. Check out the strumming logic and swing eighths lessons also, as they might help you out with this one.

INTRODUCING TRIPLETS

The triplet is all about the number three. For eighth-note triplets, we divide each beat into three even parts. Whereas quarter notes are counted 1, 2, 3, 4; and eighth notes are are counted 1–&, 2–&, 3–&, 4–&, the triplet is counted 1–2–3, 1–2–3, 1–2–3, 1–2–3. You could also count 1-trip-let, 2-trip-let, 3-trip-let, 4-trip-let. There are different methods for counting and you can choose what works for you. Sometimes it's good to accent the first note of each triplet to help you feel the rhythm and keep your place.

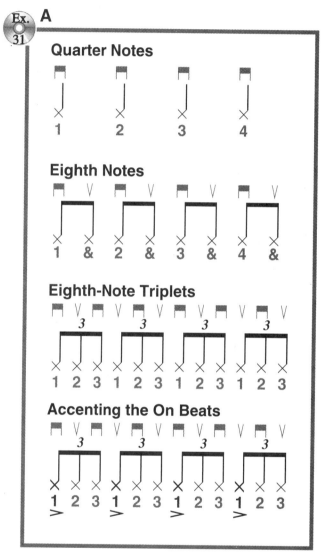

This first exercise goes through a measure of quarter notes, a measure of eighth notes, and then a measure of triplets.

Adding Power Chords to the Triplet Pattern

A really cool way of getting used to playing triplets is by jamming. We'll use the A5, G5, and F5 power chords:

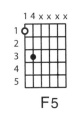

We'll add a triplet fill to each one. This is a great way of dressing up the chords, and you'll get used to the actual window of time you have for the triplet.

Applying a Pentatonic Scale to the Triplet Pattern

Triple-picking through a scale is a nice way of getting used to the triplet. We'll play a minor pentatonic scale, like example 34.

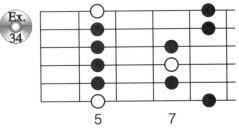

But let's pick each note three times, playing a triplet, before going to the next note.

This time, we're going to play the minor pentatonic scale straight through instead of hitting each note three times, but keeping the same triplet feel. Count to yourself: 1–2–3, 1–2–3, 1–2–3, 1–2–3, and so on like that.

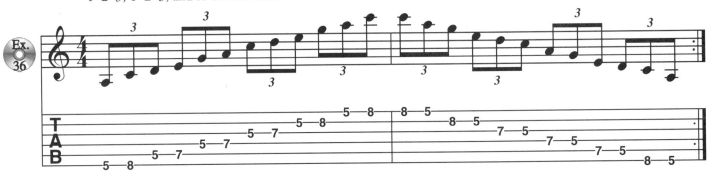

Pentatonic Triplet Licks

Here are some pentatonic licks with triplet feels. Each one of these licks is great to repeat or loop. Slow it down until you get the right feel. When you've got it and play it fast, you'll sound just like Jimmy Page.

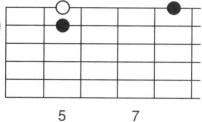

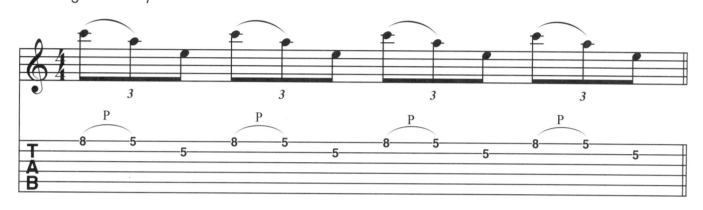

The next one is very bluesy. Again, slow it down and try to really feel the 1–2–3, 1–2–3, 1–2–3, 1–2–3. That will help you phrase the rhythm correctly.

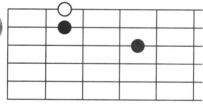

This one sounds a little more broken but still has a triplet feel. Slow it down and feel the 1–2–3, 1–2–3.

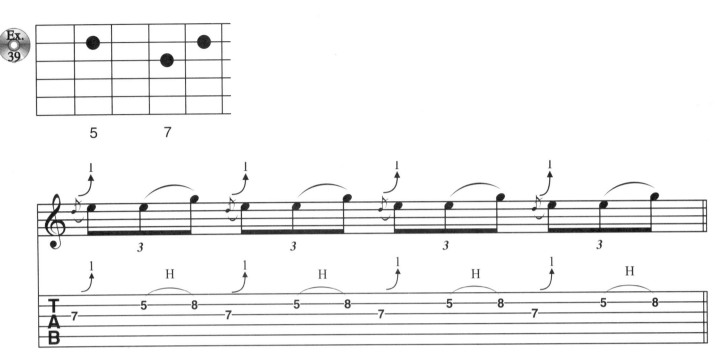

Triplet Arpeggio Patterns

A triad arpeggio has three notes in it, and so does a triplet; it's a match made in heaven. "Canon in D" is a cool classical piece by Johann Pachelbel that works great with arpeggios on the guitar, plus it has a triplet feel. Each arpeggio is played four times. The arpeggios are diagrammed below and the music is on page 23. Have fun playing this popular tune!

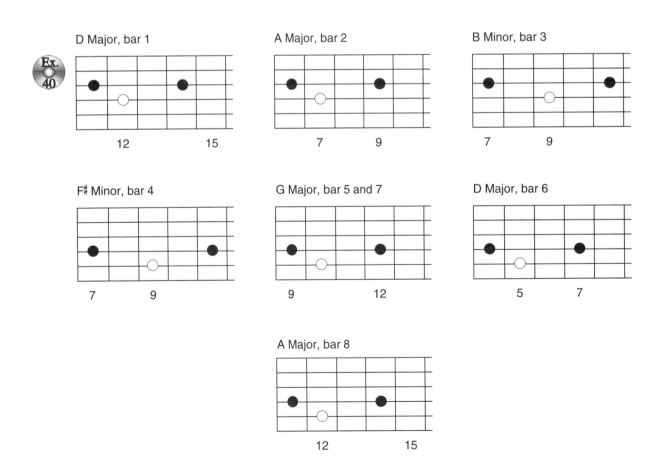

Canon in D

Johann Pachelbel

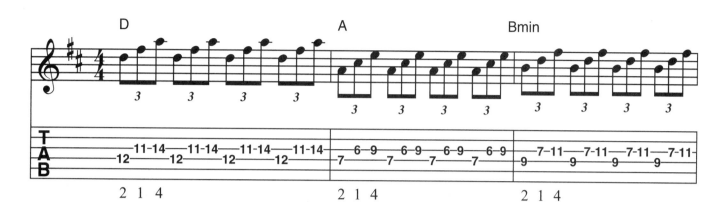

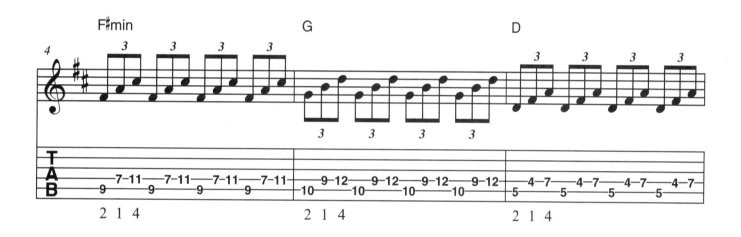

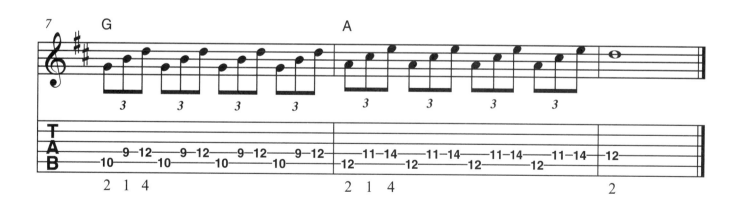

Swing Eighths

If you want to jazz up your rhythm playing, you've come to the right place. We'll be taking a look at how to *swing* eighth-note rhythms through a couple of bluesy rock riffs and some single-note soloing. If you like classic rock guitar playing, this will be right up your alley.

THE SWING FEEL

When you play *straight eighths*, the time between the attacks on and off the beat is perfectly even, but when you *swing the eighths*, the first eighth is held for longer, while the second is played shorter. It sounds like a triplet with the first two notes tied. Think of it as a stutter or a skip in the feel of the lick.

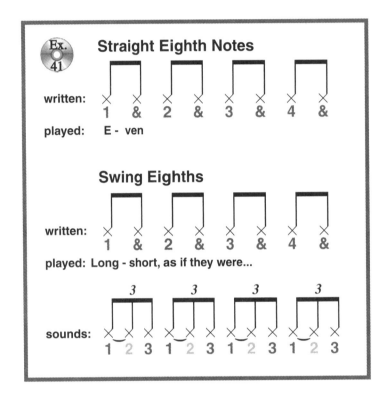

Play through this bluesy rhythm pattern twice, the first time with straight eighths, and the second with swing eighths.

Second time, Swing 8ths

Single-Note E Blues Riff

This next swing thing is a single-note riff using the E Blues scale. When you play through this example, think four notes at a time, with the first note being a fretted note out of the scale, and the other three being a pedal tone on the open 6th string. Remember to stretch the first eighth in each pair, and play the second note quicker.

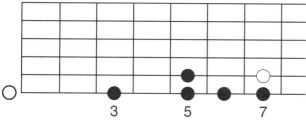

Swing 8ths

Swing Eighths Applied to an A Blues Line

It sounds great to swing on the blues scale in a lead guitar solo. If you listen to classic rock bands like AC/DC or ZZ Top, you'll hear how naturally this rhythm fits the style. This lick also has some triplets, which complement the swing feel.

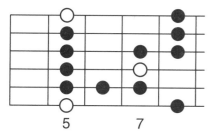

Swing 8ths

BLUES SOLO USING THE SWING FEEL

One thing I like to do when I practice is play a little rhythm, followed by some licks. The next example does just that. It will bounce between a swung open-string rhythm part, followed by some licks from the blues scale. Remember to keep the swing feel throughout the whole example, and notice that there are some triplet rhythms in the licks as well.

There are a couple of licks that deserve some special attention. The first is this double-stop vibrato figure on the fourth beat of bar 3. It is a very common minor pentatonic or blues scale gesture.

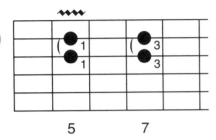

There are also have some unison bends in bar 4 that move out of the blues scale pattern.

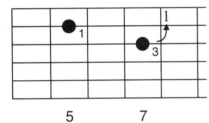

And last but not least, we have those notes from the blues scale used in the triplet licks in bars 5 and 6.

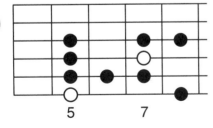

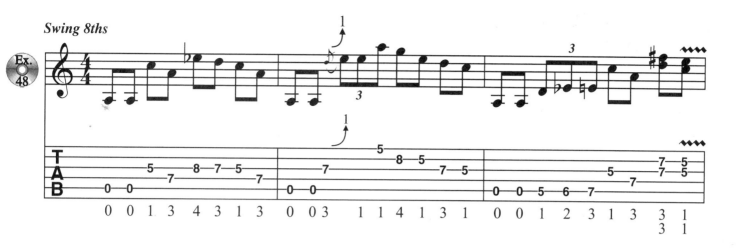

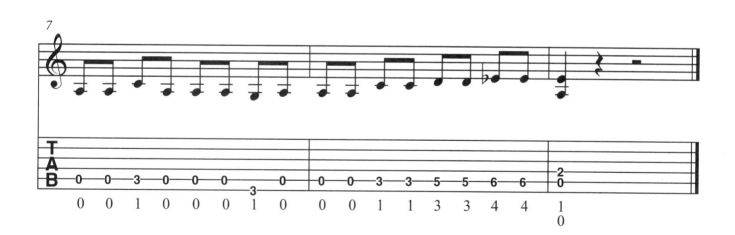

Playing this way is always fun and will definitely help get your eighths swinging.

Extra Swing Eighths Practice

Example No. 1

Swing 8ths

Example No. 2

Swing 8ths

Fingerstyle

Fingerstyle will definitely add some class and drama to your playing. This lesson will cover a couple of right-hand fingering patterns and some different approaches to using this technique. Once you get this way of playing down, you will instantly be able to capture the listener's ear.

ASSIGNING FINGERS TO STRINGS

We use abbreviations to indicate the fingers on our picking hand. The letter *p* is used to indicate the thumb, *i* is used for the index finger, *m* is for the middle finger, and *a* is used to indicate the ring finger. These letters are based on the Spanish names of the fingers as shown below.

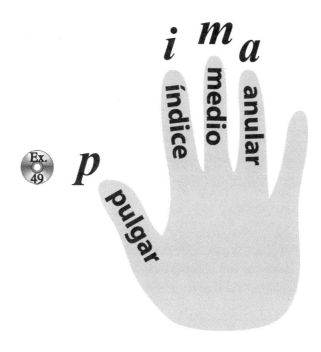

For now, pluck the 1st string with *m*, the 2nd string with *i*, and the 3rd string with *p*. Each of these three fingers is assigned a string. You can also try substituting *a* and *m* for *m* and *i*.

In this example, there is a descending natural minor scale on the 1st string, starting on the 12th fret.

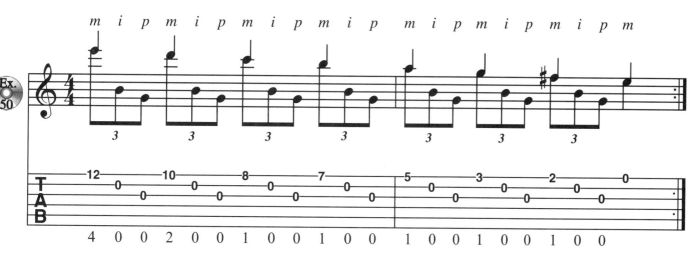

TRIPLET PROGRESSION

Now we're going to add an extra string and the *a* finger. The pattern is p-i-m-a-m-i. Notice that each finger gets its own string. This has a triplet feel, like the last example, but we play two triplets for each chord, so you can feel it in 6, like this: 1–2–3–4–5–6, 1–2–3–4–5–6, etc. The chords will be D, A, Bmin, and G.

THE DUO

This next fingerstyle technique creates the effect of duo. Your thumb plays the bass part, and your other fingers play the melody above. As you play the melody, alternate the *i* and *m* fingers, just as you would alternate between down and upstrokes with a pick.

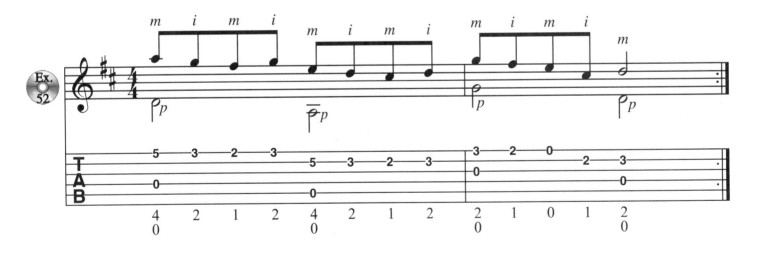

BASS AND ACCOMPANIMENT

This example combines some of the techniques in this lesson. The chords are C–G/B–Amin–Amin/G (which is kind of like a Gmin7)–D/F#–G.

Notice that *p* plays a descending bass line while *m* and *i* take care of the upper parts. Practice it one chord at a time and just get used to the pattern. Once you're comfortable, add the next chord. And of course, never forget to have fun!

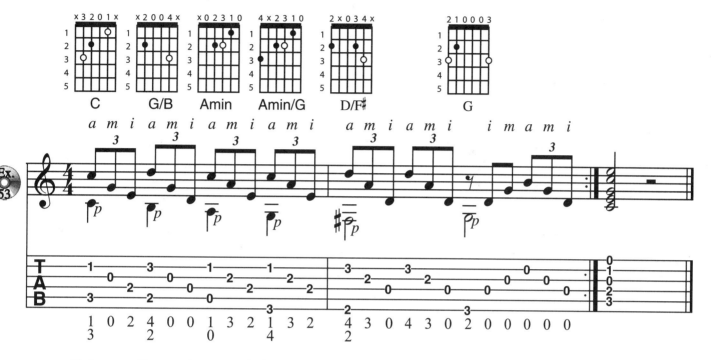

Train yourself to use the very end of your right-hand fingertips and/or your fingernails to strike the strings in your fingerstyle playing; that will help you keep an even flow and a good tone.

EXTRA FINGERSTYLE PRACTICE

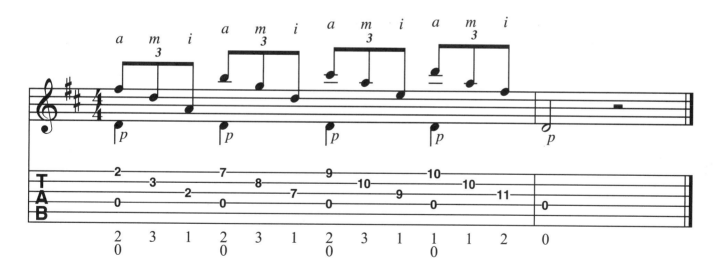

Pattern Playing

Pattern-playing, or *sequencing*, is the repetition of a musical phrase at different pitch levels and is a cool technique that will help you avoid sounding like you're reciting a scale as you solo. It's great for coming up with new licks and will give you many options for using any scale pattern without running out of notes. Think of it as number sequencing, such as 1–2–3, 2–3–4, 3–4–5, and so on, except you're doing it with notes on your guitar. In this lesson, you'll learn this technique using the A Minor Pentatonic scale.

GROUPS OF THREE

This is what I call *groups of three*: Take a scale pattern, such as the A Minor Pentatonic scale pattern at the 5th fret (shown to the right). Starting with the first note in the scale, go up three notes, then go to the second note in the scale and go up three notes from there. Then do it again starting on the third note, etc. Continue this idea until you run out of notes in the scale pattern. You'll have to keep track of where you are in the pattern so you don't accidentally skip a cluster of notes.

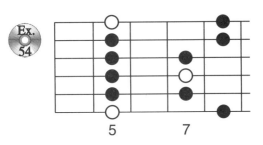

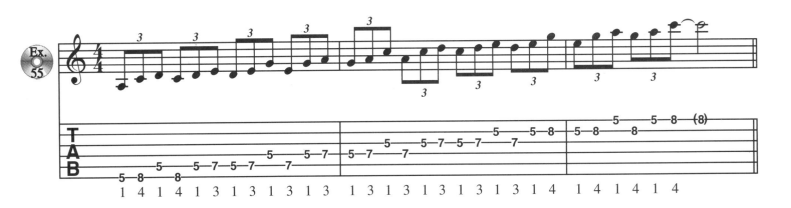

Here's the same thing going backwards. Remember to keep track of where you are in the pattern, so you don't skip a set of notes.

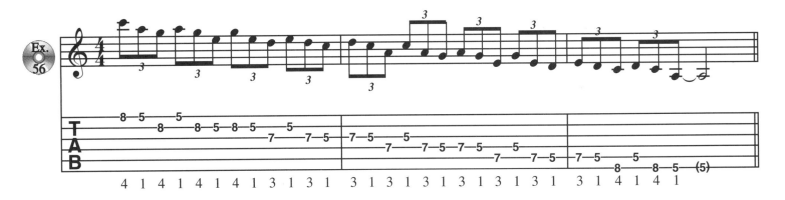

String-Set Based Groups of Three

The next example is a string-based pattern. Play all of the notes in the pattern, starting with the 6th string and ending with the 4th string, ascending six notes through the scale pattern. Then you go back to the 5th string and ascend six notes, ending on the 3rd string.

Groups of Three and String-Set Patterns

This lick combines groups of threes and the string-set pattern.

Groups-of-Four Pattern

The following lick uses a group of four. When playing notes on the same fret on two different strings (as in the end of the second group of four to the beginning of the 3rd group, from the 5th fret, 4th string, to the 5th fret, 5th string), the trick is rolling the finger across the strings. Make sure the notes don't bleed into each other, and are as separate as possible. Roll the pressure from one string to the next.

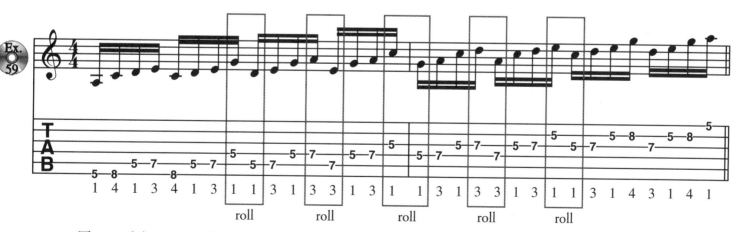

The possibilities are endless. Try coming up with some of your own patterns of threes, fours, fives, and so on. And most importantly, have fun!

Extra Pattern-Playing Practice

Example No. 1

This pattern starts on the 2nd note in the scale, dips down to the next lower note, and then returns. It is then repeated starting on the next note in the scale. Think 2–1–2, 3–2–3, 4–3–4, etc.

Example No. 2

This pattern ascends five notes and then descends to the second note. It then starts again, one note up from where you landed. Think 1–2–3–4–5–4–3–2, 3–4–5–6–7–6–5–4, 4–5–6–7–8–7–6–5, etc.

Example No. 3

More complicated patterns are possible. This one goes 1–2–3–4–1–2–3–4–5–6, then it starts again on the 3rd note: 3–4–5–6–3–4–5–6–7–8, and so on.

Other Techniques

This lesson will introduce *tremolo picking*, *tapping* with one finger, and *pinch harmonics*. These are all very cool techniques to use in your lead guitar solos. You'll get a couple examples to play with each technique, so you can start getting them into your playing right away.

TREMOLO PICKING

Tremolo picking can be thought of as a type of speed picking. The idea is to pick as fast as you can on one note. Depending on what you're comfortable with, you can use your wrist, your arm, or a combination of both. Try tremolo picking on the 4th string, using the notes shown below, just a D Natural Minor scale.

Now that you have the concept of tremolo picking, let's try a different string and a different pattern. We're going to play on the 1st string using the E Natural Minor scale, a bouncing back to the open string, tremolo picking on every note.

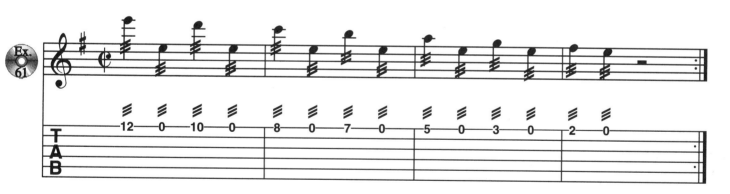

TAPPING

Tapping was made very popular by guitar hero Eddie Van Halen. If you don't know the first
Van Halen record, well, you should! The main idea is to tap on the desired fret with the
picking hand.

In this example, tap with the middle finger of your picking hand and then execute a pull-off
with that finger, creating a little friction as you would with your fretting hand. Don't lift
your finger straight up, as this might make the note go dead. Then, hammer-on with the 4th
finger of the fretting hand.

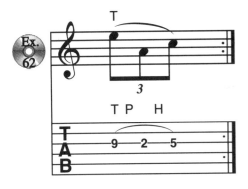

In this example, the fretting hand is going to stay on the same two frets throughout, but the
tapping hand will move up and down the neck.

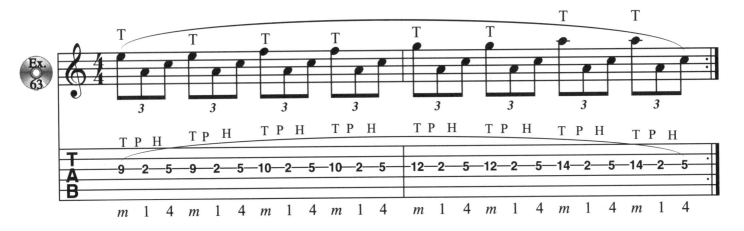

In the next tapping lick, you'll tap on just one fret, but will move across different strings. The fretting hand will stay in the A Minor Pentatonic scale pattern at the 5th fret, while the tapping hand moves across the 12th fret.

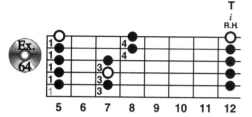

This is a great lick for adding some flash to the pentatonic scale.

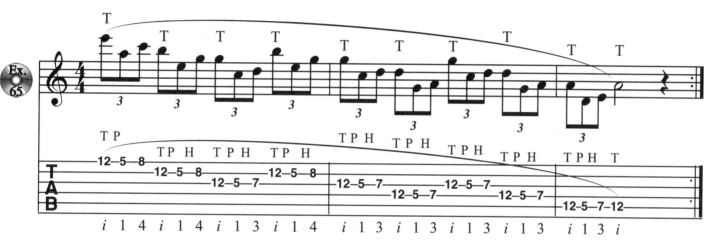

Pinch Harmonics

If you want your guitar to scream, then you've got to know how to play *pinch harmonics*. I remember trying to learn this after being told how to do it, and it took me a pretty long time before I could do it. After trying and trying and trying, it finally happened. Following is a description of the technique, hopefully it—along with the demonstration on the video—will help you get it going for yourself.

As you pick the string, let some skin from the side of your picking thumb lightly tap the string. There's a "sweet spot" on the string, so move your picking hand back and forth along the string to find the spot that sounds best.

So try playing the 5th fret 3rd string, and then the 5th fret 4th string. Very cool! It might take a little bit of time.

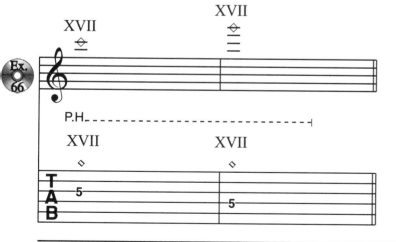

This one is a straight-up blues-rock lick out of A Minor Pentatonic scale, with a bend. Try it with the pinch harmonics. It gives it a whole different dimension!

Last but not least, you can make a more angry-, lower-sounding pinch harmonic on the 3rd fret of the 6th string. You may have to adjust where you strike the string to find the sweet spot. Play the open string normally and then the pinch harmonic on the 3rd fret. Adding a little bit of vibrato sounds great, too.

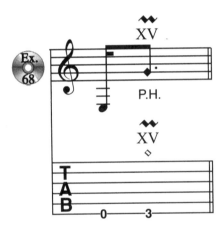

All three of these techniques—tapping, tremolo picking, and pinch harmonics—add flavor to your soloing and overall shredding technique. Make sure you master them and, most importantly, have fun.

Sweep Picking

Sweep picking involves playing a series of notes on adjacent strings with a single downward or upward motion, allowing for great speed with little work. This lesson will get you started with this technique by using arpeggio shapes that you can use immediately to make great sounding music. We'll take a look at how to do it, and how to use it.

INTRODUCING SWEEP PICKING

Let your pick fall through the strings smoothly, in one big motion, and don't let your pick bounce. The example below shows a great shape to get started. This example definitely has a triplet feel. It is an Emin7 shape.

Emin7 Shape

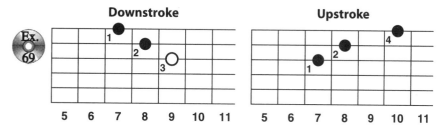

This example uses both the Emin7 shape and an Amin7 shape at the 12th fret.

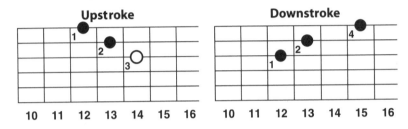

Emin7 Shape

Amin7 Shape

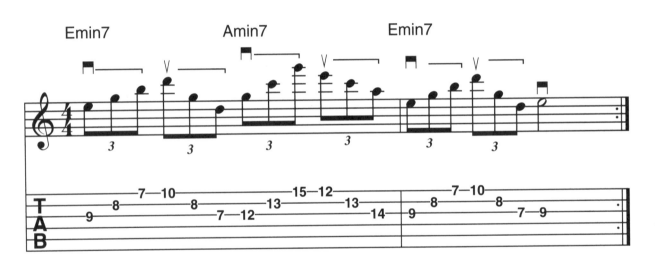

If you spend enough time practicing this slowly and working it up to speed in a step-by-step manner, it will become smoother and very fast. Take your time.

Sweep Picking Major Arpeggios

This major arpeggio shape is easy to learn. The root is on the 5th string.

A Major Arpeggio Shape

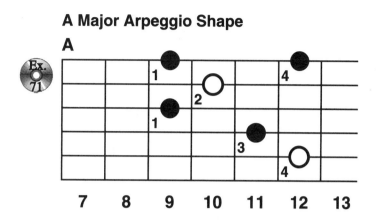

There are two notes played on the 1st string using a hammer-on and a pull-off, so there's really no disruption in your sweep picking strokes. The pattern is down–down–down–down–down, hammer-on, pull-off, up–up–up–up. To sweep an arpeggio over an A Major chord, use an A Major arpeggio.

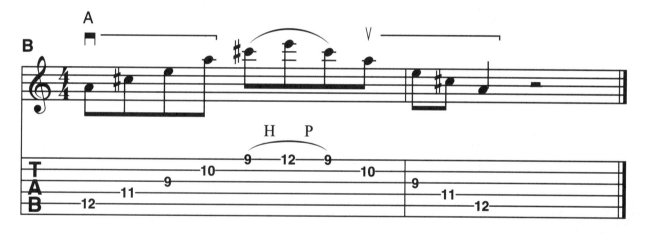

SWEEP PICKING MINOR ARPEGGIOS

Below is the minor version of the major shape you just learned. There's a bit of a stretch on the 1st string because the 3rd is lowered to make the chord minor. It may take some time to master that stretch.

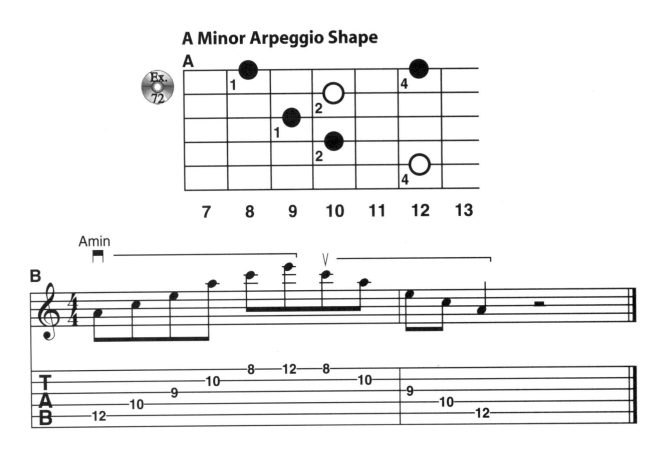

A Minor Arpeggio Shape

To sweep over an A Minor chord, you would use an A Minor arpeggio.

SWEEPING OVER A CHORD PROGRESSION

Let's put these tools to work by sweeping over this progression: Amin–G–F–E. We'll just sweep pick through each chord's arpeggio.

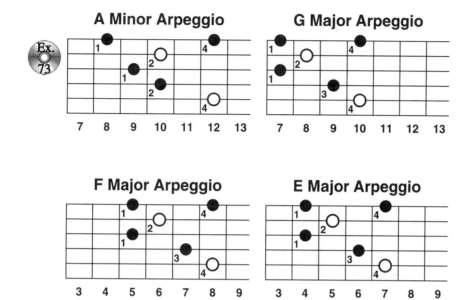

Sweep picking provides an alternative to strumming as a way of playing a chord progression.

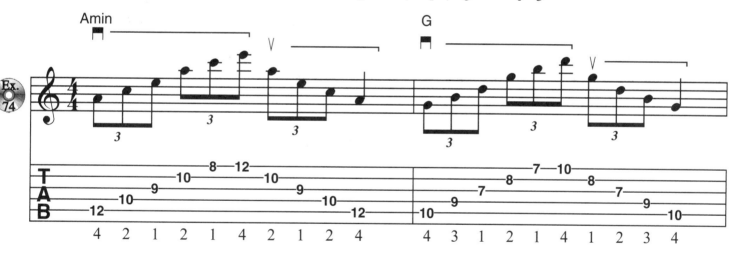

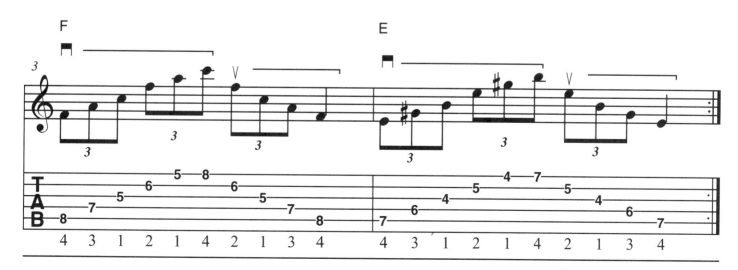

Extra Sweep Picking Practice

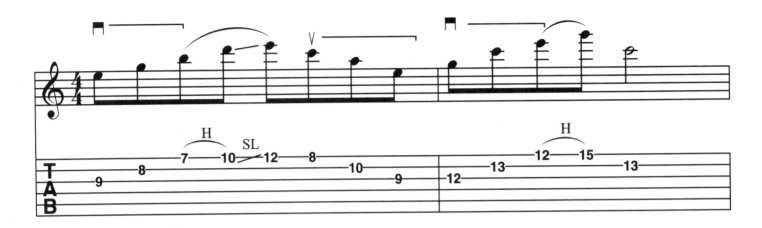

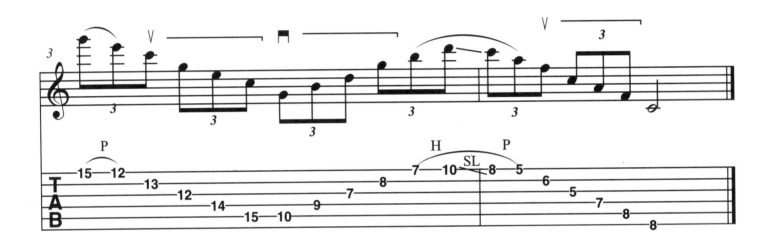

Congratulations!

You have completed *Glenn Riley's Serious Shred: Essential Techniques*. If you've been practicing and reading carefully, you have gained some important skills and knowledge. Be sure to check out the other books in the Serious Shred series.

Notes

Guitar TAB Glossary

TABLATURE EXPLANATION

READING TABLATURE: Tablature illustrates the six strings of the guitar. Notes and chords are indicated by the placement of fret numbers on a given string(s).

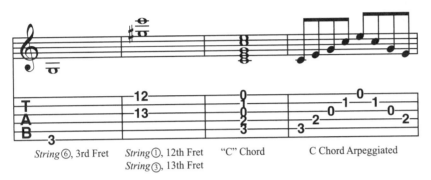

String ⑥, 3rd Fret   String ①, 12th Fret   "C" Chord   C Chord Arpeggiated
String ③, 13th Fret

BENDING NOTES

HALF STEP: Play the note and bend string one half step.*

WHOLE STEP: Play the note and bend string one whole step.

PRE-BEND AND RELEASE: Bend the string, play it, then release to the original note.

RHYTHM SLASHES

STRUM INDICATIONS: Strum with the indicated rhythm.

* A half step is the smallest interval in Western music; it is equal to one fret. A whole step equals two frets.

ARTICULATIONS

HAMMER-ON: Play the lower note, then "hammer on" to a higher note with another finger. Only the first note is picked.

PULL-OFF: Play the higher note, then "pull off" to a lower note with another finger. Only the first note is picked.

LEGATO SLIDE: Play a note and slide to the following note. (Only the first note is picked).

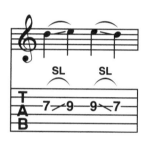

PALM MUTE: The note or notes are muted with the palm of the picking hand by lightly touching the string(s) near the bridge.

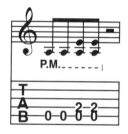

ACCENT: Notes or chords are to be played with added emphasis.

DOWNSTROKES AND UPSTROKES: Notes or chords are to be played with either a downstroke (⊓) or upstroke (∨) of the pick.